$1.85

CONTEMPORARY POETRY SERIES

CaBiN FeVeR

EDWIN GODSEY

Cabin
Fever

Cabin
Fever

by

Edwin Godsey

THE UNIVERSITY OF NORTH CAROLINA PRESS
CHAPEL HILL   1967

LIBRARY
The University of Texas
At San Antonio

CONTEMPORARY POETRY SERIES

Copyright © 1959, 1960, 1965, 1966, 1967 by Julia Winston Godsey

Some of the poems in this book have previously appeared in
*The Antioch Review, The Arlington Quarterly, The Carleton Miscellany,
The Georgia Review, The Red Clay Reader, The Sewanee Review, Southern
Writing in the Sixties: Poetry,* and *The Southwest Review.*

Library of Congress Catalogue Card Number: 67-27157

Printed by The North Carolina State University Print Shop, Raleigh
Manufactured in the United States of America

For Julia

That was the day of white rice and scarlet
Solemnities, of virgins chattering
For orchids hurled like grain against the sky,

Laughter of dark hair, wailing of gray, the bells,
The heavy fists of young men sowing seed,
The dark wine of that holy place.

Now in a winter day, a cold rain,
Now in the blessing of this table lie
Orchids, wine, and the white seed.

CONTENTS

Cabin
Fever

PETITION

We smart to hear a bird, we giddy singers
Who do not come in out of the rain but lie
Naked, gone sickly in the streaming weathers
Discharged from our own bruised, fistulous sky.

Pray for us, you. The rain is not too little
And dry to sleep but too much nightingale
To sleep decently clothed in clay and spittle,
Not naked to this pestilent flood's swell.

Devils, too scared to walk down from their mountains
Into the rain, frightened by birdsong or night,
Appalled by women's thighs or gardener's portions,
Have flapped their vans and vanished into light;

But we stay earthward in the rising waves.
We sing, for you, beneath the olive groves.

WORDS ON SUNDAY

A Chinaman squints at birds with rickshaw eyes:
He hulks the shoulders in his great flop coat,
Squints his squinted, sun-fattened eyes and sees
The birds that wing from right to left, slanting
Into a paddy-field. The Chinaman
Smiles and moves his round head vertically.

(The birds are feathered, I believe, and brown.
But I have never lived in Arkansas
Where there are fields of rice—whatever they mean.
I have seen blackbirds wheel above the marshes
At Reelfoot and a dozen sprigs or mallards,
Drakes and Susies, wing down into the blind.
That was duck hunting.)

                              Just now! . . . Do you see?
Here is a blue jay hops across our lawn
Under the hackberry tree, cocks his head,
Pecks and pecks through bluegrass, dead leaves, lifts
The long beak and swallows a hackberry. This is the
Certain extent of our communication.

I am no lookout through the middle region
Or muddy earth between us. Neither is he
Who squints in China through the sodden earth.

Where there is no love we are earth's architects.
We build it, Victorian clapboard gothic, in
Eyes without definition bird after bird,
Constructing great-hearths, roasting guinea hens,
Toasting our feet when it is winter, even
Descending stairways flight after flight to bring
Up brilliant wines for celebration. Do you
Suppose the Chinaman hears us in the earth?

I love you. Hear me? I love you. Listen.

Next
Sunday we must attend a definition.
We will prepare remembering this blue jay.
What is it you see? graceful wing and poise?
Am I squinting my eyes and see his blank
And bitter eye?

See him?

There he goes . . .
Over the grass, over the privet hedge,
Behind the mock orange, slanting to the earth.

And there is no communion of the earth,
For we began in words, and words are neither
Landscapes or meditations. They are a wild
Creature who lives out wild in the out-of-us.
They are defined by separation. They are
Blue jays wheeling into a paddy-field.

VOYAGEURS

It would be good to be a voyageur
I think, and use the wild country and river.

He launches the bateau into the heat
Of summer, sweats out his contempt for fat

Women and factors at trading posts and seeks
His country, presently fanged—its tamaracks,

Motions of deer, night mists, the night cries,
The beaver meadows. Time is where he is

And yet, the voyageur, he drives on westward,
His strong cry ringing "Allons!"—movement onward.

The river moves, the movement at his feet
Moves in the water pouring sheer and white.

And so I pray to God all voyageurs
Have kept sane during the seasons of winter

When there is no movement and the game is gone
Out of their piddling circling of a trapline,

When the world is mostly given to snow and ice,
The walls, the arctic nights, and the stillness;

Pray they have whistled, kept the fire confined,
Carved out many small deer with their hands.

ARS POETICA

It is snowing again, while I, here in this city,
Cold, gaze at a church and think about
François Villon. The snow lies deep already,
And it's falling thick. Only a few are out.

Remarkably, as then, the winter pours
Over an evening and the sky-ribbed church
With its piers, pillars, massive oaken doors—
It weights the ivy clinging on the arch.

And under snow-shot arches Villon sang
Of time, Moloch, and the seven sins
And furtively *iubilate deo* sang
Praying in darkness he might be forgiven:

He who had roared out "Prig!" at d'Orléans,
Had knifed two Christians and escaped the guards,
Had followed drunken with the girls of France—
Those doxies whom he sang of afterwards.

He sang how Mother Church hanged men in snows
Like this: they who abandoned hope and grinned
From Mountfaucon over the city's narrow
Streets where the night blew cold and Christians sinned.

He sang it down—both devil and Christ, he said.
He sang it up—the heart's polarity.
For what it's worth, the rhyming put a blade
Into the throat of time and cut him free.

ODE IN CHARCOAL

In the cold blue of the coming night
Drizzling sweat and dew cool
To crimson feet

Wisdom an upright fool

To know the glow of fireflies
Under the summer's maddog moon
The sound
Of an old hound
Coughing it dry

Luckily almost never I
Taste the green again

The devil
           Buddyboy you are a laughing loon
To hear bugs glow
But the sound of an old hound
And cold dew whets the sawgrass blue
For crimson feet

And for the scars

Hearing silver speed
Of dewdrops flaked from the skirt of the evening star

Or was it Venus then
                    I don't imagine

To dash splash and quiver there
On sawgrass cool and green there
And mash the finger of a wooly spider

The devil
                Buddyboy do you confess you are
A rosy-eared cherubic idiot

Who has heard dewfall

But the sound of an old hound
Chops the shells of sparrows' eggs
On crooked legs
And sawgrass cold and blue

Who has heard dewfall at all

Later under the moon the horses squeal
Clear from the second pasture
As witches weave their vital manes
And from the window there
One striding tall with a straight back there
And an evil nose

                        Mamma Mamma
A witch

            Randall
Is that you
Randall
Let us sleep son
Say your prayers son
And let us sleep

The devil
                Buddyboy do you claim kin to the bat
To hear that
In the cold wind of the coming night
Are you some kin to the owl
To see a witch scowl
In the cold blue of the fading light

And the clean white sheet
Is warm
And clean
To crimson feet

MACABRE

The snowman, what can it be?
Mockery of death
Or mockery of life?
Iconography
To the child's creature joy,
The being able to breathe?
Or is its cold grimace,
Making children laugh,
The grin they make him wear,
Mockery of a face
We found in the grade-school picture?

I have known a housewife
Grapple her hips to laugh
At the grotesquerie—
Why, call the neighbors out
All ages in a rout
To swell the mockery.
Have known grand-dad bring
Pipe to stick it in
The snowman's awkward grin
Then jig back to the ring
Of those who laughed at that.

Woman fetch a hat
The husband wore last year,
Tilting it over an ear,
Above the coal-lump eyes,
The yellow carrot nose.
Schoolgirl merrily
Twine her scarf to rest
Upon the snowman's breast
White as the fleur-de-lis,
Roguish as they shout,
All ages in a rout.

Other tricks are done
In winter under the sun.

However, I suppose that
Mad Napoleon,
If he were ordered straight,
Would not celebrate
This winter ritual
—Unless the thing were stone.

Probably Aristotle
Would prove us if he could
During a morning stroll
His golden attitude
Toward this ritual.

Perhaps the Elder Brueghel
If he were here would lay
Perspective on the way
To view this ritual.

Perhaps Amos Fitch,
Scott County's water witch,
Divined this ritual.

Jesus, He would know
—If there were enough snow.

EUPHROSYNE

Poor soul, past the dark trail and a broken stone
Carved with the name that would not signify,
By the time we found her she was too far gone,
And no one knew how she had got there or why.

Our universities had joined the search, but
After the third day they had had to resume
Verbals and declinations of stars, and yet
The kids would shuffle their feet in their narrow room,

And one intelligent young man in the front row,
According to the girl who could see his face,
Mumbled, gazing toward a classic window,
Mumbled, as though it were over an empty space.

So when we brought her out the traffic jams
Backed up for miles, the city's offices
Emptied into the streets, and telegrams
Poured in out of the farthest consciousness.

By night we had had the wolves and little sleep,
Rocks, pythons, laurel thickets by day.
But we pushed on, till we were in so deep
We found the gorge where this crazed woman lay

And did our best. Even the foxes came,
White and red, lovely under the trees:
However, as she failed they turned the same,
Snarling against their old enemies.

So wild was there, and green, and so the human
Speaking a name, trying to bring her to.
Finally one of us said it felt like rain,
And we started out the way we had come through.

She had lost contact. You know how it is:
As the anesthetist numbers you down
You fall and fall colder than the sea is,
Beyond Orion and beyond Orion.

A TOUCH OF FREEDOM

Smoothly along the sinews in his mind
And down the meditative turning wrist
His true and rolling perfect line unwound
Until the Coachman fly and pool had kissed

And wild with human kinesthesia struck
Exactly through the cold reflection on
Water bright as mirror until luck
Broke wild and the feel of the trout was gone.

THE IDEA OF THE HOLY

At sundown he drew basins of the fatted
Calf's blood, stirred in the usual wine and grain,
And sprinkled it richly on the flaming, matted
Nest of the half-mad phoenix in his brain.

At midnight, then, he poured a cup of milk
And left a penny for what bearded elf
Might quit his tricks, his mountain, and his ilk.
He slept before the pixie showed himself.

At daybreak, having warmed the crucifix
With his flesh, he took flesh (and, later, grapejuice),
Praying the grisly devil feared crossed sticks,
And praying his dear father might burn loose.

He mixes lather now. The basin fills.
The simple suds reek sweetly in his nostrils.

THE FOWLS OF THE AIR

They talk, talk and talk about concentration.
What I want is ease. Do they think a hawk
Is willful when the talons strike and tighten

Into the bittern's wing after the sweep?
Or that a fixed idea or fanatic
Fever drives the rider toward the leap—

Feeling the withers move and turf flung loose
To roll the line fence under and the bite
Of the calks? A rider must be easy in it.

The ease of it, the riding in control
Beyond one's efforts or the riding school—
O, I will sweat but find this emptiness!

That is what Adam said when he began
Hoeing his beanfield at the break of dawn.

A CRIME IN THE CITY

Not even Samuel Johnson took his punk
In Watling Street, not even Wallace Stevens
Confronted the other but in his own mind.

Boone would whisper, "Kentucky!"

                                    Before the event
The young woman had kept a Persian cat and
Goldfish, the man had blinked his eyes among
3,000,000 others and had chosen night,
The uninvaded streets, *Lebensraum.*
Picasso wrote the commentary on Malthus.

At a lunch counter next day the physician
Stared at his broccoli like Boone at the fire.

SPELL

Is this the end of learning:
To comment on the burning
And image those inside,
Thinking how they died?

Always to abstract
The motive from the act,
The object from the prayer,
Being self-aware?

FOR GRANDFATHER CORNS (1852-1936): THE PURITAN GRANDFATHER, SOUTHWEST VIRGINIA

What were you dreaming when you memorized
Paradise Lost? (Your daughter Lynnie tells it.)
Did you, grave, cloudy grandsire, fume and spit
Cobpipes of Heaven's wars at firelight? late prized
Eden till midnight? Chaos realized
In burley smoke, and a dottle of Hell? Nitwit,
Didn't you know Chaos and epic fit
Would send a child to sleep quite mesmerized?
    And she still sleeps, fleeing the baleful nightmare.
But I do not dream I fly away. I do.
I have climbed higher than a Puritan.
I have winged down on valleys from bright air.
I have wheeled over where the roots go through,
Where your stained skull compounds with earth and rain.

FOR GRANDFATHER GODSEY (1829-1897): THE MOUNTAIN GRANDFATHER

And were there bearded men who don't make sense?
Who fought the Yankees, voted—Clay had died—
Republican, sawed timber, roared, and forbade
Their children to play mumble-'e-peg o' Sundays?

Bless you, Grandfather. You rode clean across
The mountain to Virginia's Wilderness
And tasted sand until you sat so bony
Your bones cut through your buttock in the saddle
On the last spring ride home.

                No. You don't scare
Us with your saber. We the logical
Have hated little. We have loved the hawks
Swinging at Tinian or Berchtesgaden,
Have pledged our pesos, rubles, yen, and pence
For Rex, a covey of birds, an orchard fence.

SUMMIT CONFERENCE

Mountjoy! they cried, and steel
Sheared, guts were ribboned, men
With a certain joy fell,
Certain the world was then.

Above the Moral Will,
In sudden hit or miss
We have climbed up to kill
These dozen partridges,

And earth and heaven should
Be glad we make a toy
Of what was neither good
Nor bad, only Mountjoy.

HOPPY

When Mary pulled the sorrel's reins from Stephen
The stunt man's hands, swung her buckskin squaw's skirt
Over, leaned up into his neck and by God
Was gone, Morris began shouting: "What are
You doing? Is she ruining me? Cut!
Hey, Sweetheart! Somebody grab that woman. Cut!
She shouldn't be galloping in it here! Cut!"
I was the camera jockey on this series.
We took her last frames going over the rise.
Guitars were to volume up there for *The End*
With boys back here all lithe as cats, leaning
Against the fence and singing "Tumbleweed"
While Hoppy turned, waved, and rode away.

It was his riding off like that that got her,
I guess. It must have made the girl forget
Hoppy was phony. It's hard to understand, though.
She'd been around. She knew the camera angles.
You would say this one had quit pulling taffy.
One time I took her out myself. Just once.
She was O.K.—a little hard is all.
But that was back before they disappeared.
Way back before the war. You never know
About a person. Some people get mixed up.

I could have used a Hoppy—Oh, my God—
At Anzio. Oh, you'd have been great, Hoppy,
The way you jingle-jumped from boulders, bullets
Whining in ricochet but plugged your ten
And came out clean ("Move in for the close-up, William"),
And gee-whiz coursed the outlaws through the hills,
Leaped on them horseback, rolled into the gulches
And whipped them silly in the sound effects.

Maybe she thought he was the real thing or
Something like that. It's hard to understand, though—
Conestoga wagons, whiskey brawls,
Gold miners, Sioux with smuggled Winchesters
(Who'd take your scalp), the gunfights at high noon.
But she was safe there, even in that wild land.

It's interesting to think what they said when
She caught up with him. Hoppy would grin and nod:
"You keep a sharp eye out for Indians, Ma'am."
And she, "At last, I've found you, Hoppy. Hoppy,
I love you." "But Ma'am," he'd say, "no epic heroes
Have time for love—I mean, the family kind.
I can't be different. It's mostly killing here.
A hard country, here, to live in." "Better,"
She'd say. And he, "But this is no place for a
Woman or child." "Why it's a good place, Hoppy,
A good place. We'll have sons—trust me—more than
The sands of the desert. And every one a hero.
I've seen the signs." "We ought to make camp soon . . ."
(What could he say?) "You understand you'll have
To keep a sharp eye out." They'd build a campfire,
Drink coffee, eat sourdough hotcakes, and hear coyotes.
It wouldn't be as easy as a motel.

So all in buckskin love went riding on
Somewhere. At least they never reappeared.
Old actors say they ride the desert still
(At times they see a family resemblance
In one of the young crew but never so soft-
Spoken or beautiful as Hoppy was)—
She and the hero with the tall black Stetson
And easy grin of a boy, on the white steed.
They say they ride toward sunset by the mesquite,
Through the arroyos and beneath saguaros
That stand like giants in the land: Clip-clop,
Clippity, clippity, clippity, where the dust
Splashes like pools of water from those hoofs,
And twilight coming on in El Dorado.

It's nice to think like that, but what I think is
They ran into trouble at Los Alamos
Back in the forties, and needed to move fast
("Ma'am, what in hell is that?") and didn't make it—
And lost the way I lost at Anzio.

IN SPIRIT AND IN TRUTH
(For Rachel Carson)

Remembering the mammoth's eye
Gleaming, heavy lidded,
Catching the sunlight as she swung
And trumpeted and bobolinks
Scattered to either side
Into the verdure:

Remembering the mammoth's eye
Sparkling, glinting,
A crystal, dendrite of earth,
And the conjunction of sunlight,
Cloud form, grass lilt, apples, the smell,
Bobolinks, the mammoth's eye as
You hurled a final javelin and
She trumpeted, blood pouring,
Shuddered finally:

Remembering the mammoth's eye,
As it takes the essential conjunction,
Is real, objectively so, truth,
Being, eternity:
It may save your soul,
Remembering the mammoth's eye,
And apples,
How your father read to you
On cold nights
In front of the log fire
After the milking . . .

Remembering.

As you drive down the asphalt
Between the beer cans, coke bottles
Dead opossums, dogs
Into the expenses,

It may give you a place to get hold
In truth,
Make a beginning,
You, the new Thomist.

AMERIKA

They say it was on a steep down-hill grade
That Betty, Roland, and the children took
The wrong exit on what was a new turnpike
Up at the upper right-hand corner and
Parallel with theirs at hand but to the left
Very close up—obliquely crimped in at
The meshing at about 60 mph

VALLEY FALLS ROAD: NEXT EXIT read the sign.
The lettering was white on forest green,
And it clearly read, VALLEY FALLS ROAD: NEXT EXIT.

So then this lettering began to spin
Into the daughter's kaleidoscope, turning
In unrepeated fragments, the cool grasses
Of fields and shadings of line trees, the horses, plowmen,
The sense of movement. Maypops were growing rank and
Butterfly weeds in the fields, the trumpet vine,
A thousand ox-eye daisies, sunlight. A white
Sky-triangle piece fell to the lower left.

And so that day the rider with the easy
Wind-swept handlebars met them at the crossing
And Betty leaned over Roland, screaming above
The wind's roar: "Sir, we are on vacation. Would you
Direct us to the VALLEY FALLS ROAD exit?"

That young hood leaned into the handlebars
And, wrapped in the plastic jacket, cried out, eyeless,
Grinning, waving them on:

                    "Man, you gotta go!"

EPILOGUE: THE WILDERNESS

Patches of moonlight mark a bound
Of pinoaks. Here frost gleams like foxfire.
A bluetick whimpers and tries the air;
The hounddogs sniff the frozen ground.
And you and Briley speak your chances—
Already hear the cat, the death-row
And gun. But sharper comes your breath now,
For the tan bitch sounds and, snarling, dances
Hard on her leash. "That way! She's struck!
Unsnap the dogs!" After they whip loose,
Spread, and then straighten on the chase,
Briley, he coughs, "God give us luck."
For this is the fabled cat, a brute
Who't bit six calves clean through the neckbone,
Who springs like plague beneath the moon.
She'd yank your steeltraps out by the root.

Turning to Briley, you curse and say,
"I swore she'd never get away."

You hear the hounddogs take the beast
Against Flintrock, and though your back
Is sweating, hair gooses up on your neck
To hear them tongue an end to this quest.
Your tan bitch whines at the cat's turning
Like one whose litter has begun.
She circles and then hurtles in
Straight at its mouth, claws, spitting, girning
Under the dark cliffs, where so precise
The green flame strikes and now so swift
A paw that hound and bowels are cleft.
While the bitch screams, you swallow ice
And pump three flat-nosed slugs. It's done.
The pack goes in. The land is well.
Briley, he shouts "She's beautiful."
Cat and hound writhe. The green flame is gone.

Turning to Briley, you laugh and say,
"I swore she'd never get away."

Oddly, you picture your wife Ann—
Transfigured, face flushed at the stove
While coffee perks for her cold love.
Proud is her greeting, you imagine.
But then—"I'll carry the damned thing out."
You kick the snarling dogs aside,
Shoulder your trophy, and let it ride.
You think, "It will scare her to see the cat."
But fearing neither this nor ghost,
Ann climbs to see how your son keeps,
Yawns, shivers awhile, and sleeps.
At first, perhaps, she is far, or lost,
And next she runs to her dead father
Or suddenly screams at some dark face,
Screams, and so turns a child's white face
From beast, from blood, the old accuser.

Turning to Briley, again you say,
"I swore she'd never get away."

FOR WILKIE

Perfectly knit by patience, luck, and water,
We waded to catch red-eye in the river.
Wilkie, another strike? Yes, but I missed it.
You'll hook him next time. Yerked to the purling water,
While swallows dipped to dimple and fly free from
Our river swealing rock but not us there.
Our flicking wrists made no weft in the whorl then,
Assuredly no warp in our green river,
No woof. I got him! I got him! That makes a dozen!
Big as your hand, hard, like cold silver,
Vital as flint—O, eolithic treasure—
From our green river under the sun. Perfectly
Knit by luck, patience, and the flowing water,
Spun in the river and our quiet chatter.

ONE FOR CAROL PETERS

The afternoon had swung
Around our point and ran
Harder than two young
Foxes on the plain:

Laughing—it was good
To hear you laugh to be
Racing from the wood
And there no memory—

You crossed the quiet stream
And lost, and you hound my head
Like all the dogs of time
Gaining, coursing red.

SEA OATS

If I were a cavalier of harmony,
A minstrel of the gittern ecstasy,

A priest of roses—any doubtless one,
I would take you and gather the old sun:

Mindless in heaven we. But I am not
Such a tall boy apt for ideal riot.

We will reap sea oats, Love, between the sand
Sea beaches and the forested mainland.

HORNPIPE

We caught the seagulls flying in
Des Moines, veering downwind, upwind.
Smelled sea winds, smelled
Seaweed beached in Iowa.
The ocean rolled over, and pounded, rolled . . .
Difficult keeping soul
And body together in Des Moines
With seagulls. For over an hour I spoke
Wisely of trout and clipper-ships
Doing a hornpipe.

ONE FOR THE ROAD

I laid no siege and brought no 3-ton ram
To starve you out or batter in the door.
You didn't need the cannon where I came.
You knew, honey, I was no chevalier.

So our Great Troy was won with espionage.
I paid for the drinks, whispered, found my traitress
And so with her assistance wired the bridge.
The mayor wept, reading the press release.

But every burg has got its ruins—its gout
In suburbia, pleuritic factories,
Malignant slums, thrombosis in Main Street.
The slabs go down on crowded cemeteries.

Woman, there were nine strata of Ilioses.
Helen's was burned. The others fell to pieces.

THE YOUNG INHERITOR

Only the young inheritor
Whose home is to be drowned out in
Some great impoundment could know how
It was. There was no more to say:
Nothing for me, nothing for you.
Fields, quick river, hills . . . the home.
But he must turn away.

PERSPECTIVE

Pausing at the edge of the lawn, he shivered
In the damp night air. There would be a frost
Tonight to kill the jonquils blooming along
The drive and hedge. The hedge might save them. Oh, well . . .
He shrugged and stared a long while at this house,
Hugging himself against the chill, moving
His feet a little like a weary dancer.

Lifting a clenched hand then and sighting down
The thumb, he focused the light from the windows,
Which dazzled, the way he saw it, spiraling
Above the windowframes and over the roof
And even into the trees like a five-alarmer.

How would they find the new town? How would it be?

Oh, well . . . He decided it was time to go in
Out of the dark and walked on to the door.

MOUNTEBANKS

Polka-dotted, nose-blotched, white-skinned, flap-shod
Sad-faced and green-haired great grinning clowns clamber
From the A-model into floodlights onto sawdust
At the center ring under the Big Top between
The lion tamer and trapeze artists while
The elephant riders go around and around—
Clamber and the red A-model explodes, fires
At them, and so they whoop and howl and prank.
A yellow dwarf with shoes and breeches too long
Pulls down the breeches of a lean, pink one
Who snaps them loose on the orange galluses
To bare the scarlet underwear. "Another
One's crawling out." "Why, he must be eight foot
Tall!" "He's on stilts!" "How in the name of God
Did he get in?" Scattering elbows, popcorn,
A boy sings right out loud: "Look, Pa, nineteen!
I counted nineteen! I counted nineteen clowns!"
But wound from the trapeze ladies, rages the father:
"Heck, son, it's just a trick. They practice. It's only
A trick. They's nothing to it. They learn how, Bud.
They all dress up like fool clowns, and they hunch
In there." Astounded by his father's keenness,
The boy marks them again, intently—to
Recount the clowns, to make certain. The little
Girls are all laughing. It is the greatest show
On earth. The band is playing waltzes, and
The elephant riders go around and around.
Neither does Mother think on Jesus now.
She is laughing. She is fat and she is laughing.
Mountainous, hot-dogged, calicoed and popped
And Baptist, her belly hurts her so, but she
Can't quit, she cannot cease, she cannot stop it—
Bulging against the waistband. "Oh Lordy! Oh Lordy!
Those clowns!"

I suppose it is all legerdemain.
The right hand has turned loose. They hang like monkeys
And mock themselves inside the cage, or outside—

Fling peanuts to their anthropoid despairs:
They kid the yokels, and they scorn the clowns.
But it's a keen show, in spite of this—graces,
Disciplines here, if legerdemain, that are
Not in it there, beneath the relatively
Honest stars. The elephant riders go—

"Boy, have you ever saw a hoop-snake?"

                                        "No, sir."

"They roll up on you and they sting you, dead."

"Mama sent me to get a can of baking
Powder, a card of buttons, and a pound
Of coffee."

                    "You think you could outrun a rubber
Tire was a rolling at you downhill?"

                                        "I guess not."

"You hurry home now, boy, before sundown."

"We're going to the circus tonight. You going?"

"A hoop-snake creeps out hungry. And you ain't got
A chance."

                    "I ain't studying hoop-snakes."

                                        "No.
You get on home now, Bud, before nightfall."

The valley flamed with dragons on the way.
Dragons lie coiled outside the Big Tent, but
The elephant riders go around and around.

What in God's name am I doing up here? The clowns
Are all like puppets down there. Dear God, is this

A puppet show? Is this four hundred feet?
—Like puppets! What am I doing here?

"Ladies
And gentlemen, the greatest show on earth
Presents, in answer to your popular
Demands, the death-defying act, without
Benefit of clergy or safety net, the trapeze
Artistry of Alonso and Simone!"

Alonso? Simone? What in the world is this?
What in the world? Alonso and Simone?
Say, is that you, Simone? old girl? And say,
Have we met whirling above the dark monkeys
And rotted sawdust at our perilous height?
Or have I seen you by the bed of childbirth—
Where the physicians go around and around?
You seem more arrogant than any stallion.
You toss the mane upon your neck like any
Stud horse in timothy. It's a long fall.
I am afraid. Dear girl, don't horse it now.
No monkey business now. Be human now,
And we will let it go in the discipline
Of now. Do not consider the poised, sculptured
Diana or the point of balance of
Discobolus. They are unreal. They have no
Meaning but in the tautness and release
Of us. Do not imagine future cities.
They have no being—Memphis and Wichita.
I do not hanker, now, for sleep tomorrow.
Here, I am ready. And the show's up to us.
We know the discipline—the lithe perfection
Of never there but here, the calluses
And cold steel of our legerdemain. Let it
Go now. Simone, Simone, hold on tight.
Ah now, now. Turn now. Here now. We got it now.
The clowns are pranking in us and the boys.
Our old friend Jack, the lion tamer, lives also
With us. The band plays waltzes in us and
The elephant riders go around and around.

Certainly we will fall and die. They will
Crate in more sawdust, use the shovels, place
A notice in the papers saying we whirl
With all those beneath the more honest starlight.

WISE ENOUGH

So he has made a trellis for her on
The downhill side so that she will have
Roses and, before it rains and at dawn,
The smell of roses. So he is wise enough.

I HOPE I DON'T HAVE YOU NEXT SEMESTER, BUT

    before you step out
    Aphrodite
    honey
    hold your ear down close to the conch
    and see can you make out
    any
    noises.

ALLISON

Heralded by trumpeters and cried,
Beaded with sweat, the armor jangling,
Their great studs shuddering, they rode
The compass of the green in order.
Then they held before the throne.

One by one he had named them for her—
That old one, that great one the sun, and
Clouds, sea oats, breakers, pipers
And sanderlings, umbrellas, children,
Ketches, the green sea ridden silver
In order. The games awaited. She

Yawned, Our Lady Allison.

STILLNESS: AN ECLOGUE

I

Miss Savage, the gnarled cliffs, the rain that fell
Silent under the spruces, the brows of spruces
And blue eye of the sea, rain and the still
Fjord that you dream of with you there

Small on the bones of cliff above the sea—
Have you traveled to Norway? Where is it now,
This fjord where you were? And in the moment
Of your death gasps, where will this fjord be?

II

Even in the formal garden, yellow flowers
Express sunlight—heavy forsythia
And winter jasmine lined before the walls,
Textures of crocus, grouped japonica,

And jonquils focusing the aims of walks—
Yellows express the meaning of the sun;
Even the evergreens, the box and ilex,
Are never still but crumble in your fingers.

III

The statue at the center of the garden,
The statue of our young Diana with
The arms uplifted in her hardened breath
At the center of the pool at the center of

The college campus. She has the stillness of art:
A man's perceptions burning, man's perceptions,
The hall of mirrors reflecting the reflections
From sunlight on the fjord by the farms

Of Attica. What stillness she contains
Moves in the twisted hands of his despair.
The stone she stands on is our better altar:
Though beneath us, it fulfills itself. It is still.

IV

Ice-out destroys, crazes, breaks loose and
Plunges. It uproots the natural scene,
Splinters the red-oak and the balsam; it
Loosens the river. Boys come out to stand

On bridges that tremble, lean out over the rail
To watch the young colt go. Next winter there
Will be new stillness, but now, in this classroom, I
Am washed beneath the current of the river.

V

Miss Savage, after you receive the degree—
Supposing you get it, what will become of you?

I will be married. I will have fine children and
A fine, warm home. And I will love my husband.

But who will be the dreamer of Norway then?
What being will you make before the children?

No dreamer. I will grow wise and teach them. I
Will love—to the best of my ability.

But in the nightmare and the trivia
Will you ponder the better stone, even Diana?

I say I will take comforts of sun and rainfall.
I will grow sweet and wrinkled as an apple.

Perhaps. Perhaps. But this will not suffice.
We build an altar to some notion of stillness.

I will be married. I will have fine children and
Be warm in winter. I will love my husband.

DAY IN SCHOOL

Some of the items in this series were
Items already linked, already programed
In nature's cybernetic time, a few
Also in man's, although our blinking time
Structures do not prove cybernetic, program
No blossom histories, the cards fall out
Far otherwise. Here then are the items:

Angling between two smooth brick paths that moved
Like me except in a less blurry focus
Toward Science (classroom building, Gothic), I kicked
Through scattered elm and oak and maple leaves,
Through shredded pieces of leaves the boys who rode
Leaf-shredders plus two or three good frosts had left
Around. I was supposed to teach them Shelley's
"Ode to the West Wind" that day. Sure enough,
A tolling of the bell scattered kids slowly
Out the building and down the steps, across
Campus beneath the winter elms, maples
And oaks. All carried their intelligences.
All spoke their words in the wind. None of them ran
As though racing before the wind. None shrieked.
Two spectacled, crew-cut young men looked
Me in the eye, grinning, and spoke, and one
Young lady smiled with the benevolence
Of affluent co-eds who say, "Good morning." I nodded.

In long-sleeved sweaters, knee socks, in their madras
Jackets, in gaily colored skirts in plaids
And tweeds, colors, flashes of eyes and lipstick,
They came—the girls and the gangling boys. They whirled.
They drifted, swept the campus, scattering in
And out, many funnelling down one path
To pile against the coffee shop, a few
The other path toward dormitories. My thirty
Angled with me toward Science for an hour.

We talked about Shelley's great ode—new birth,
Climbing beside a mountain stream, finding
Its rhododendron banks with their wild blossoms
Strewn by the rain, eddying in the pool.
We talked about our own machine, about
The categorical imperative.
You had to wipe the baby's nose, to do
Your children justice. They hoped this would lead us
To no more or final murders. I agreed.
We talked about their time. I said that I
Hoped they were living in their time, paid
Attention to their time. And they agreed.
We gave ourselves a full hour of our time
To Shelley's poem strewn by rain, eddying
Beneath the rhododendron banks, I guess.

Contemporary Poetry Series

Edwin Godsey was born in Bristol, Virginia, in 1930. He received
bachelor's and master's degrees from Vanderbilt University and
earned a doctorate from Yale University in 1961. He taught English
at Vanderbilt and at Centre and Converse colleges, and became
associate professor of English at The University of North Carolina
at Charlotte in 1965. His poetry has appeared in *The Antioch
Review, The Georgia Review, The Sewanee Review, The Southwest Review, The Carleton Miscellany,* and *The Red Clay Reader,*
Edwin Godsey died in 1966 while attempting to save one of his
children from drowning.

The University of North Carolina Press   **Chapel Hill**

Woodcut by Janet A. Howard